ONE BABY JESUS

This book belongs to

_____

ONE BABY JESUS

WRITTEN BY Patricia A. Pingry

ILLUSTRATED BY Wendy Edelson

ideals children's books.
Nashville, Tennessee

ISBN 0-8249-5511-0

Published by Ideals Children's Books
An imprint of Ideals Publications
A division of Guideposts
535 Metroplex Drive, Suite 250
Nashville, Tennessee 37211
www.idealsbooks.com

Text copyright © 2005 by Ideals Publications
Art copyright © 2005 by Wendy Edelson

Color separations by Precision Color Graphics,
Franklin, Wisconsin

Printed and bound in Italy by LEGO

The Library of Congress has cataloged the boardbook
edition as follows:

Pingry, Patricia.
    One baby Jesus : a new Twelve days of Christmas / by
Patricia A. Pingry ; illustrated by Wendy Edelson.
    p. cm.
    Summary: The birth of Jesus is presented in the pattern
of the familiar "Twelve Days of Christmas."
        (alk. paper)
    1. Jesus Christ—Nativity—Songs and music—Texts. 2.
Christmas music—Texts. [1. Jesus Christ—Nativity—Songs
and music. 2. Christmas music. 3. Songs.] I. Edelson,
Wendy, ill. II. Twelve days of Christmas (English folk song)
III. Title.

PZ8.3.P558678 On 2001
782.42'1723—dc21

                            2001035209

Designed by Georgina Chidlow-Rucker

10 9 8 7 6 5 4 3 2

For Abigail

On the
first
day of Christmas,

my mama gave to me

one baby Jesus

sleeping
peacefully.

On the

second

day of Christmas,

my mama gave to me

two parents

smiling

and one baby Jesus

sleeping peacefully.

On the
third
day of Christmas,
my mama gave to me
three wise men
giving,
two parents smiling,
and one baby Jesus
sleeping peacefully.

On the
fourth
day of Christmas,

my mama gave to me

four camels
plodding,
three wise men giving,

two parents smiling,

and one baby Jesus

sleeping peacefully.

On the
fifth
day of Christmas,

my mama gave to me

five golden

stars,

four camels plodding,

three wise men giving,

two parents smiling,

and one baby Jesus

sleeping peacefully.

On the
sixth
day of Christmas,

my mama gave to me

six donkeys

braying,

five golden stars,

four camels plodding,

three wise men giving,

two parents smiling,

and one baby Jesus

sleeping peacefully.

On the
seventh
day of Christmas,

my mama gave to me

seven shepherds
kneeling,

six donkeys braying,

five golden stars,

four camels plodding,

three wise men giving,

two parents smiling,

and one baby Jesus

sleeping peacefully.

On the
eighth
day of Christmas,

my mama gave to me

eight angels
singing,

seven shepherds kneeling,

six donkeys braying,

five golden stars,

four camels plodding,

three wise men giving,

two parents smiling,

and one baby Jesus

sleeping peacefully.

On the **ninth** day of Christmas,
my mama gave to me
nine lambs
cavorting,
eight angels singing,
seven shepherds kneeling,
six donkeys braying,
five golden stars,
four camels plodding,
three wise men giving,
two parents smiling,
and one baby Jesus
sleeping peacefully.

On the **tenth** day of Christmas,

my mama gave to me

ten cows a-**mooing**,

nine lambs cavorting,

eight angels singing,

seven shepherds kneeling,

six donkeys braying,

five golden stars,

four camels plodding,

three wise men giving,

two parents smiling,

and one baby Jesus

sleeping peacefully.

On the **eleventh** day of Christmas,

my mama gave to me

eleven doves **a-cooing**,

ten cows a-mooing,

nine lambs cavorting,

eight angels singing,

seven shepherds kneeling,

six donkeys braying,

five golden stars,

four camels plodding,

three wise men giving,

two parents smiling,

and one baby Jesus

sleeping peacefully.

On the **twelfth** day of Christmas,
my mama gave to me twelve hugs and kisses,
eleven doves a-cooing,
ten cows a-mooing,
nine lambs cavorting,
eight angels singing,
seven shepherds kneeling,
six donkeys braying,
five golden stars,
four camels plodding,
three wise men giving,
two parents smiling,
and one baby Jesus
sleeping
peacefully.

The Real Christmas Story

Luke 2:1-16

And it came to pass in those days, that there went out a decree from Caesar Augustus, that all the world should be taxed.... And all went to be taxed, every one into his own city.

And Joseph also went up from Galilee, out of the city of Nazareth, into Judaea, unto the city of David, which is called Bethlehem; (because he was of the house and lineage of David:) To be taxed with Mary his espoused wife, being great with child.

And so it was, that, while they were there, the days were accomplished that she should be delivered. And she brought forth her firstborn son, and wrapped him in swaddling clothes, and laid him in a manger; because there was no room for them in the inn.

And there were in the same country shepherds abiding in the field, keeping watch over their flock by night. And, lo, the angel of the Lord came upon them, and the glory of the Lord shone round about them: and they were sore afraid.

And the angel said unto them, Fear not: for, behold, I bring you good tidings of great joy, which shall be to all people. For unto you is born this day in the city of David a Saviour, which is Christ the Lord. And this shall be a sign unto you; Ye shall find the babe wrapped in swaddling clothes, lying in a manger.

And suddenly there was with the angel a multitude of the heavenly host praising God, and saying, Glory to God in the highest, and on earth peace, good will toward men.

And it came to pass, as the angels were gone away from them into heaven, the shepherds said one to another, Let us now go even unto Bethlehem, and see this thing which is come to pass, which the Lord hath made known unto us. And they came with haste, and found Mary, and Joseph, and the babe lying in a manger.